STARTLED NIGHT

ESSENTIAL POETS SERIES 184

Canada Council   **Conseil des Arts**
for the Arts   **du Canada**

ONTARIO ARTS COUNCIL
CONSEIL DES ARTS DE L'ONTARIO

Guernica Editions Inc. acknowledges the support of the Canada Council
for the Arts and the Ontario Arts Council.
The Ontario Arts Council is an agency of the Government of Ontario.

ELANA WOLFF

STARTLED NIGHT

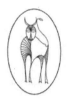

GUERNICA
TORONTO – BUFFALO – LANCASTER (U.K.)
2011

Michael Mirolla, editor
Guernica Editions Inc.
P.O. Box 117, Station P, Toronto (ON), Canada M5S 2S6
2250 Military Road, Tonawanda, N.Y. 14150-6000 U.S.A.

Distributors:
University of Toronto Press Distribution,
5201 Dufferin Street, Toronto (ON), Canada M3H 5T8
Gazelle Book Services, White Cross Mills, High Town, Lancaster LA1 4XS U.K.
Small Press Distribution, 1341 Seventh St., Berkeley, CA 94710-1409 U.S.A.

Typesetting by Antonio D'Alfonso
First edition.
Printed in Canada.

Legal Deposit – Third Quarter
Library of Congress Catalog Card Number: 2011925132
Library and Archives Canada Cataloguing in Publication
Wolff, Elana
Startled night / Elana Wolff.
(Essential poets series ; 184)
Poems.
ISBN 978-1-55071-348-0
I. Title. II. Series: Essential poets series ; 184
PS8595.O5924S83 2011   C811'.54   C2011-902153-6

CONTENTS

FOR MENACHEM

You must change your life.

Rainer Maria Rilke,
"Archaic Torso of Apollo"

*Before setting foot in the Holy of Holies you must take off your
shoes, yet not only your shoes, but everything; you must take off
your traveling garment and lay down your luggage; and under
that you must shed your nakedness and everything that is under
the nakedness and everything that hides beneath that, and then
the core and the core of the core, then the remainder and then the
residue and then even the glimmer of the undying fire. Only the
fire itself is absorbed by the Holy of Holies and lets itself be
absorbed by it; neither can resist the other.*

Franz Kafka,
"The Third Octavo Notebook"

STARTING WITH THE CARDINAL

Brought to face value. Mitt-red. Tail flame.
Nothing to say but singsong and it's shrill, shrill,
brilliant. The peonies, unfolding,

smell of old-world birthday rose,
pink underclothes. I count them
while they're up, I say Seidel –

Seidel, Seidel, for every head. Then they're
down, unfazed as earth. Intimate in messiness
with the snail trails on the flagstone –

cue to the holes in the hosta leaves,
glue of genus helix with its golden ratio
home described by phi. "i" in the spiral rising,

I fall to the lawn. Languor in its blades. Sun
hammers me all over with candescent beams
and horns, flashing up that Sistine figure of Moses.

WATERWHEEL

A wet man loves the sea he's knelt in,
how the salt enlists his skin
and lingers till he bathes and dresses,
rinses his mouth out with water.

*

It's 1999 again
and nature – clouds, the Sound, the slough –
submitting liminal signals.
I don't know what they say exactly,
only that I am parched.

*

Rain colliding
leaves against the window: autumn blotto.
The pummelling of trees so freely
leaves me tipsy too.

*

An image comes to mind – a yard and rails,
an empty bench. A cantilever bridge,
a rainy river – the voice I hear
announce its name, *fortissimo*,
revives me.

*

I have a new life, it's the same life,
the same name, it's a cognate –
as in firmament:
     sky
from which the seas were taken.

CONVERSATION

I make myself only as constant as clouds, says she.

      Contradictory as water, says he.

Restive air,
convertible earth.

      Accomplice of the cosmos, you mean.

I'm not clear about that – if it happens by grace, or chaos.

      Maybe through the merry march of nature.

Ah yes, nature. The essential traits.
    – I took my cue from your tongue.

      Those midnight songs on my pawnshop guitar?

The guttural thrum.

      What about my essay on the origin of birds?

That too. Spirit needs futurity, and an encrypted past.

      Harps and Angels.
      Kettle drums.

When you locked on my gaze through the classroom
    door,
I saw our course, reflected on your cornea.

     – You were blocking the exit.

Vigilance I've always kept for deeper, nearer mirroring.

MOONSHINE

I was in the state between sleeping and waking –
slipping like a baby out of bliss to the place
of naming. Dipping back and forth – from the couch
where I could hear the hum and bubble
of the fish – to where I saw myself unstructured,
before the premise of sex. Buffered somehow,
joyful as a beck – both carried and carrying.

The only image I was able to moonshine
back to the world of waking, making, division
and dread was the counterpart of carrying.
And insofar as it is an image – no beginning and no end.

NAKED FIFTH

Painting is the silent stroke,
open/close.

Black the jalousie louvering white; light
the lip of time.

Dark distills in death, the living
night is unrefined.

First the image, then the word; bird
and then abode.

Plover, plover, lose your "p".
Land and make a play for me.

HOKEY POKEY POEM

Fetal weight: your fatal weight.

Seven holes to the human head:
one for every day of the week.

Close your eyes and plot
the sunspots' tenebrous reprise.

Where the haunch is at its thickest:
there go in and go there through.

The key to heaven's happiness
is lowering the portal.

Children don't recall
the names of streets; they know

the smell of sheets, the way
from bath to bed

to school;
they learn the looby-lie to looby-loo.

TWO BY TWO

The year our parents parted – first de facto,
    then de jure, out we moved
from the nuclear, two by two.
    The guinea pigs and gerbils died, the cat

fell off the tenth-floor sill,
    the talking budgie
flew into the mirror over the sink.
    Pets like these don't live for long –

my sister offered solace. She understood
    how quickly matter scatters.
I heard the cry of
    every time I'd slapped her on the back,

the days I'd been the wicked
    bigger sister,
and was sorry; practiced reparation giving orders:
    Bring me milk, I'd say;

a mug of milk would appear in my hand.
    Shut the window,
lock the door. Both were quickly closed.
    Draw the blinds, she drew the blinds.

Turn the night-light on and come to bed.
    Hold me, I would say,
and we would reach across the gap –
    holding tight until we nodded off.

I brought so many
    acts that year
about by fast command, I actually
    began to believe I could conjure the future.

YEARS LATER, ASHBERY

Eight or nine years old, you see
    a young wife slip and topple off
the sloping concrete
    walk beside the building, you are up above;

hear the husband cussing,
    see her baby-belly wobble as she fumbles
and she tumbles.
    Did he push her? Did he see you see him

lift his yo-yo eyes at you? Does she
    cry or lie there, quiet,
caught between the curb and truck –
    the angle from the balcony's oblique.

You have to lean beyond the rail to view
    the Humber River and it always makes you
swoon. Dean Martin on the air is crooning
    That's Amore and below you someone else's

love you've glimpsed or have you glimpsed
    another story tucked in yours.
Children in the courtyard chanting –
    One, Two, Three, O'Larry –

notice nothing of the husband,
    how he yanks his darling up
and shoves her in the truck. Kicks
    the curb and pins you there

where everything goes Whoa.
    Honest little body
eats her macaroni dinner, cleans her
    teeth and goes to sleep. Dreams of endless

meadowlands, of downy clouds and flower
    beds, shiny water spouting out of alabaster
ground, mother hugs and singing kisses
    first thing every morning –

all that's pure and pleasing in a child-mind.

DAMAGE

What child hasn't stuck a hairpin into an outlet
to probe the hole.

You can't undo it, even in ink.

It soaks your clothes, the muddle: woad.

The ladder to the attic adds to the caveat –

       the way it does with things once fun.

Can you even call it fun, though – when it's this un-
hinged, hiss-continuous.

A spleen pervading my dreams got its way
and took to day, found the double: seat of meanness –
       black concocting
adder-black beneath.

I heard the sound of whetted metal –
       slow slicing,

  honed and low.
It could have been something harmless, I know.
But damage was patent,
       champing to happen.

STYX

I'm walking up from Oakbank Pond
escorted by a bat – dipping overhead

in the dusk like a drunk. Daddy praised
his mother as the loveliest hurt in the world,

Granddad had a murky slough-blue marble
for an eye – the real one drained by fate.

This morning we were wakened by a hornblast
from the street, last image in my dream

a waning gibbous. I've died a hundred times
but something big keeps bringing me back.

Truck called *Licorice*, boat named Styx.
Black Negligée – the cimicifuga –

blossom-rods of honey draw the wasp.
As remedy for moods like this, I go

for the long lone walk, step ahead, my
standard mantra: Happiness is a dactyl.

ON EDITING

Pencil in
corrections and suggestions.

Mint for her my words, misread/her writing,
mine, the merger. Her memories/

mine, the mix. Overlapping Catherines,
hypotheticals, a foreign friend,

from whom I learned a visionary word –
seer – as vague and veiled at twelve as

quasi modo. New girl with the Lamp Black
hair and Esmeralda dresses, tiny

pearl pierced-earrings from Bombay.
Pierced, for me, is not allowed;

I ice my lobes to pull the sewing
needle through in secret. Turn the doubled

thread each day to keep the holes from closing,
till I save enough for studs.

Gold so bold, remote, so near, so pearly-near
my lobes they show the error of my way –

one stud always higher,
one stuck
lower than the other.

DOUBLES

Amongst the lianas at Tortuguero.

Lanterns light the path, wet air envelops.

We've seen fireflies for the first time
illuminate lacunae, heard howlers, mynahs,
touched a dead gecko. Eaten hearts
of palm in dish after dish.

Father and son adventure ahead.

Mother and daughter, loving the mist,
                                        go slowly.

The pathway blackens with huge armed ants.
Shade-glow. December of them.

One version of the story has the ants attacking,
pincering unshielded feet.
High hysterical screams.

Another way of putting it: the men are off.

Either way, mother and daughter are not.

In every sense, I feel blood of my blood.
Between pincers and relative skin,
I am as localized as pain and panic.
By some overlapping sharp-point in our bodies,
I know I can kill.

I ask you:

Minus our doubles, are we half-ourselves?

Less each-other.

Being three-dimensional, can we be shadowless?

HAMMERED FRAMES

Night-sky lidded, sleep about to
buzz with what will be in the dream:
Leigh's suspended legs – erect-to-the-clefts
like Ezekiel's angels; her deep-set eyes –
blue beryl wheels, and human mutable beauty
spark and tenor of electrum.

> I was shy the day in group we hammered frames
> for stretching paper – lay the wood across the table,
> sopped the *Fabriano* with water, drew it taut
> and fastened it with tacks. Leigh showed us how to
> wrap the corners flat as origami, and after checking
> mine, chirped, You must be good with gifts.

I see her in the dream, deplete –
force fire from her irises,
leak green through hollow feet.

> Long ago, in front of the class, I read a story
> containing her name, enunciating it clearly, to rhyme
> with *sleigh*. Our dour fourth grade teacher corrected
> the error, my classmates laughed. She asked me to repeat
> her and the ceiling instantly lifted. From somewhere up
> above, I parroted, *Lee*.

VEIL PAINTING

Hooded, hatchet in her hand,
a swan in the negative space –

stand away and squint to see it framed –
ice-white as the

lake from land-to-island, middle winter.
A greyish halo circles sun,

its outer ring a faint full-spectrum
rainbow. Call it glory.

Venus in her rich mobility
centres you in green and you are

heartened. What do you do with love
but lean? Strength is in the yielding,

pathos the pith of the poem.
I liken us to flowers, therefore:

St. John's wort, euphorbia.

PHTHALO

Sky on the drive back from Bloomfield –
      did you see that mother of space?
All fraught and fired, feral.
                Greet and tear,
billow and rip. Wind nigh and shifty,
              shining,
     clouds concocting
teeming creatures out of cumulus
        and nimbus: salamanders,
sylphs,
     amphibian wings – titanium white:

      I'm bringing them to tempera
mixed with linseed
oil and egg,
pressings of hibiscus – *Disco Belles* as big as faces.

      Helena says I've opened into
Odilon Redon – his gravid shadow
surging in the flatness of my canvasses, some
noteless soul-song fluting into ash-
chrysanthemum, blackened cadmium,
     phthalo blues,
and roses.

HELLEBORUS

Hangdog
        head, hamstrung
heart, she bends to the faun-smelling
earth for the comfort of dirt.

        Were there no
        real demons
she could quickly decide on light.

        Wind clicks,
        shadows split
and spill
through quirky trees:
        Glyphs and sigils.
Sigils and glyphs.

The sun in her blood is not enough –
        she leans to heliopsis,
        Lenten Rose;
sinks her fingers into the soil,
        taps a glassy surface.

Slowly, over the hour,
        works a window
        out of the earth.
Soap veneered to its panes
congeals the view.

LEMNISCATE

1

I sit at the bench on the deck. Thighs-to-iron,
feet-to-flagstone; eye the early summer yield:
cherries, still-green damsons, apples,
lavender, basil, mint. The billowing arctic
willow waving paganly over the fence. Potentilla,
spiraea, pink syringa, spurge. This is my address.

I step from the deck and knee the even earth
beneath the cedars, check the empty robin's nest;
set upon the colonizing sumacs, seize their shoots.
I have to take them out. They crowd the other shrubs,
choke their roots. I bag the fuzzy suckers and expel
them to the curb. Before the damsons ripen,
                              they'll be back.

Stage of the raven: bare.
Whatever she envisioned: flipped.
Whatever she considered –
switch. The audience is not concealed.

There is no audience.
Raven stage is bare.
Sometimes you can hear the bear.
Here before he eats you and

you enter a rcfrain.
Like law in claw,
loss in gloss,
Julia in Giulia.

You enter and contain:
hoof in beef,
victor/victim,
lemniscate in circle.

Green as plums in June,
raven is black, naturally shadowed.
The cherries that mantle her tree –
red as her reveries of cherries.

PARKER'S POINT

We pedal across the lake to *Daisy*. Rhythm in us,
water wheels beneath our boat and soles.
Damselflies ride piggyback in bluish hues and twosomes,
                              hover at our hands.
Whitewash on a shrub at the tip of *the island* marks the
     target –
above, two huge blue cormorants are preening on the
     tree-peaks;
                    we're lapping in the lee.

What comes up and up in me is innocence, then pleasure.
Sun a raging saint, his burn already in my skin.

FISHING WITH DEAN BARLOW

We went down to the zipperlip
with our one, two, three little wishes –
hooks, lines, sacrifices

and summer-solstice time.
Sat there at the water's edge
and waited for the fish. I didn't know

how little a boy could have to say,
but his fingers were pretty nimble
and he hooked the bait for us both.

I felt his breath; it stunk of mud.
At least it seemed to be his breath –
could have been the water-hole,

earthworms, or the bucket.
From the side of my eye, I saw
the sketchy freckles on his nose –

blurred to watery blots.
Not like mine – all separate
and peppery. His arms

and legs were skinny-long,
soft blonde hair on his shins.
I saw this, too, from the side of my eye;

looked askance at my own shin hair
and wanted madly to hide it;
tucked my legs beneath me, making it

hard to hold the pole. Dragonflies
skimmed the water, shimmering pink
and evening-blue – so beautifully I forgot

my legs, our freckles, and the stench.
And in the tug of a simultaneous catch,
the bone of our strangeness broke.

MANICURE

The day I gave you a manicure
you sat across from me like a tall
toy soldier, quiet as clay.

I used a glass ashtray for the soapy
water and held your
hand under mine

to soften your nails.
This could have been a time
for revelations, as such times often are

between beauticians and their clients.
But I am not a beautician,
and you are not a client.

So we sit in perfect silence.

The only sounds are the snip of the
clippers, the back-and-forth of the file.
We don't make eye contact,

so as not to exchange superfluous words.
And when it's over, we sit there for a
minute more, still as the big steel

juicer on the counter in the kitchen,
after I turn it off and it comes
to a slow, centrifugal halt.

RE: COLLAGE, SEARCHING FOR A NAME THEREOF

Midsummer, end of Regine's course. Here I am
digesting the work and I'm wiped. You'll find me lying
in the swing – the cedar hedge beckoned me out.
So thick and big at least five kinds of bird have been
seen in its greenness. We are born to make each other
sing. You hear the birds chirping to their young
just as we coo to ours.
        We might be running on kairos time –
past, present and future joined by heart and invisible
sutures. Fuse and bloom. The bark of us, the rose and
lily, dandelion-seed and echinacea. The back of us,
the black, its shine, the sound behind the *Salvia* –
divinorum. Why do you laugh when I'm being
perfectly frank. If ripping and tearing and working
on the colours of the others had happened anywhere
else, it could have been ugly.
        No. First we must be ugly.
Unskilled. Upturned. Undone and inside out.
Blue. So that the yellow-red glows orange.

HIERARCHIES

Sun the husband. August, strong.
All Leo long he's shone this way. Consequently
earth is thirsty – arid, unattractive. In-
side another wife is standing, mulling at the sink.
She turns the water on whenever she wants.
Wash, to rinse, and drink. Her neck and temples
dewy where the seeds of sweat collect.
She lets her memory loose,
and pool,

        go simple as a fish – whose days abate
in rhythmic pulsing: swim,

    feed,

hide. The kitchen window wall-eyed.
She views her duplicate visage in the green
beyond the glass, framed by arborvitae,

        apple,

           sumac.
Birds there know a few new tunes
they learned from flying skyward

      where hierarchies

sing in berths of blue.

UGLY STUFF

We're not to vaunt our luxuries.
There are appearances to keep under wedlock.

Conniver is the moniker she likes to
                  use on others.

How do I tell her how many times she's told
that same old jape.

A pain shoots through my nape.
                          That same old saw.

If we have them, we're not to speak of them.
                              Not flaunt.

The porcelain quota:

We enter through the backdoor, usually used
                    by gallery staff.

Set our ugliest stuff on pedestals.

It's not as if these monkeys'll gather dust.

                The subway shunts and rumbles
                      underneath us;

subtle gets jumbled to *sublet*,
"*s*" slips off and lands before *laughter*,
thinking devolves to *ink*,
             feeling to *eel*,

and the lion lows as the monkeys hump.

FROM THE GROUND UP

Sifting for some interlinear gist.

A stand of silver linden trees in hills of broken
                                    shins and knees.

We're visiting a glass chalet.
In the vapour-light of morning the windows look
                                    phantasmal.

The host conducts us to the deck
to view the drop and mountaintop –
                                    shade and elevation.

   As visitors we're not authorized to talk.

I look into the slope below and focus on a form – a
squat and waddling
brindled thing, shunting a stump like a mate.
It rockets out of the valley
suddenly halts before my face.
                  Wriggles in the air – suspended –
solid brown now
ogling me,
         its snout a mask,
                  a flail – I'm frozen to its gaze.

                        Gradually,
               losing levity, it de-
      materializes.

The Überwurts are harmless, quips our host,
dismissing the incident. They wriggle to try
and get you to flinch, but only strike if you move.
Naturally, he puts to me, through overweening teeth,
You knew to hold your pose.

It is morning and I have my pride – *von Grund auf.*

AUBADE

A woman went for a walk at dawn and came
to an iron bridge – high, yet in the river
below the sky appeared
so close. As if she could have

stooped and touched its hue. By the river
stood a wood of densely-fretted firs.
For years she'd longed
to fall, be caught.

How beckoning, she thought,
and off she leapt.
The branches broke
her fall. Winded,

she returned to earth.
Not a soul had seen the leap,
nor the ragged landing.
She met a man with a camera

on the path back into the city.
You're wearing fir, he laughed
and asked if he could take her picture.
Sun arose, prodigiously,

and rinsed the heavens red –
he fell to his knees instead:
How would we stop from bowing
down, if the sky were always this vermillion.

EMBOUCHURE

The sun grows garish,
then gaunt. A fading orange organ
in the bedroom,

embouchure.
This is the way you've come to me this evening –
in a box, on the wall, reflected.

Lodged
in the slatted
shadows of the shutters,

then not even there.

Before the orange ebbs completely,
into the autumn night and
you abscond,

I strain myself to listen
for a tune
of your affections.

And one comes up from the loin of my tongue,
like muddy
waters onto my lips.

Though this could be a phantom too –
spectral as
the gases of Uranus.

TWO IN RALUCA'S WAITING ROOM

> *He drinks my colour*
> *like a moon and cackles*
> *as the stars*
> *on the mountaintop*
> *dance red.*
>
> Thomas Bernhard
> *Under the Iron of the Moon*

We hear the muffled voices from the room
beyond the anteroom and strain to tap
the psychic's magic accent. Minds go light
from time to time with waiting but the air
here's thick – so old with smoke it fills our
heads with Camels. *He drinks my colour*

in, his eyes go green – these moving hues:
Helio Medium, Chromium Deep, Kelly,
Cobalt, Lily, Leaf. A slide-show: my projection.
What does this man see, if any shade at all,
in me? We utter nothing. A gull alights
on the sign outside, *like a moon and cackles*

language past the glass: Everything for you
occurs in twos – who is he speaking to?
Must be me, the Twin, and yet this other
looks so dual too. We shift and fidget, fidget,
shift and reach in sync for a magazine
as the stars shine up from the glossy, dog-

eared cover. Fingers inadvertently touch. This
could be the start of conversation, but it's not.
We snatch our hands away at once; neither lifts
the magazine. I rummage in my purse instead,
put my glasses on and gaze at the painting
above his head. *On the mountaintop –*

it's Kilimanjaro – a splat of something ruddy
has dried in a runnel. If it weren't solidified,
it'd travel down the canvas, over the frame
and land on this man. This is what I see it doing
now.   The splat returns to liquid, flowing down
Uhuru Peak – Rose Pink, Scarlet Lake, *Dance Red.*

POINTILLISTS

The morning starlings
bank above the hornbeams in a
pointillist
mass, cross the vault of thin-ribbed heavens,

      fall,
becoming ink.

I think of sin – how you
insinuated infidelity
into the openings in my poems.
Poked,
      drew close
enough to the holes

           to find albino
irises blacking back at you
as asterisks,
full stops.

ALCHEMILLA

Brown flowers: Lady's Mantle
lapsing into fall –
             rumpled ruff of former
                          chartreuse stars.

Poetry is in her pleats,
                   utility her beauty –
she holds the rain in droplets on her sleeves.

Medievals called this saving-trait: reprieve.
         They made a strong decoction of her roots
to cure wounds,
                   tincture to untangle sleep.

The shimmer-myth,
              imbibed to heighten life
and fetter fears,
is folded in the creases of her cloak.

WICKS

1

Fall in love, it's water wicking
deeply up the wall –
          separateness dissolving.
Wall, wall, wall, seeps water, *Saturate.*
               Completely.

2

Nature's paint completing evening:
pinkish brindle, mantis-mauve – skyline
dying into indigo.
                    Long ago
a boy and girl, dark of an empty
apartment. He'd lived there till a week before
and still possessed the key. They realized
this was trespassing, and huddled – still as
wicks. Backs against the wall, breath shallow,
knees tucked taut to their oceanic chests.

3

It thrills to think of outage – failure to power,
eye of the storm. Electric
light bamboozled at the source.
Candlewicks a windfall then. And wax,
a book of matches.

4

The scar – a pearly sliver,
glowing glitch – refracts the night.
      No matter how white the starlight,
how mollifying the moon – their shining
on the memory tenders, *Wicked, wicked, wicked.*

5

Torn pine, wishbone branch
of hailstone-broken oak, western hemlock
baubled blue. The bailiwick: year's end.
I'm walking and the airiness bears me;
thinking over and over of direction,
and progressing; stopped before the light
by a small mauled creature at my feet.
Missing skin, two perfect frozen teeth.

WOODPECKER IN CAPRICORN

I might not have seen him hunkered
       in the hub of the leafless shrub,
             but he shifted.
The ardent marks and needle beak
were not what attracted me most.
              It was his cap,
worn like a yarmulka tilted back: colour of luck
                 and blood.
I wanted to reach out, into the cold, to touch it.
He knew and didn't move. This was his largesse.

In the minute we stood there staring,
he at my solid body, I at his feathery head –
       earnest, gentle, circumspect –
the pond beyond us, plain as a table,
attended:
       an altar for ice.

WHAT'S BECOME OF US

I burned in the crime of having you,
drowned in the light of leaving you, we
died together jumping from the Second

Narrows Bridge and were eaten by fish –
caught in a net, trawled to a deck.
Moon-glow bathed the slippery hill

of achromatic scales. Two bodies
will be lifted from a tidy bed of ice.
Weighed by the monger before they're

filleted. The woman who selects them,
skinned, has in mind an intimate dinner
served with Pinot Grigio, no bickering.

Scraps will go to the tabby.
And far down the hallway of horrors,
someone will uncover what's become of us.

13 LUNG TREE

Writing blue custodial poems, happy
accidentals, shin-deep in a
sweetness that invokes a thin-hipped
woman wide with smiling past her pain,
holding onto life

like a bell and a kite.
                    Parts of us disperse.
I am not afraid to stay alone nights
in the vigil, though the lamplight
sputters and the floorboards

creak in tongues.
I've met with these phenomena: We built
our house across a bridge
that won't hold on to bank, or beam, or stone.
                    The other
        side occultly waits
and here the shutters

flutter. Parts of us detach,
disperse – like secondary colour.
                    Green, by law,
is leaf and won't adhere for long to firmament –
the yellow has a way of lifting up
and streaming out, leaving
        sky a primary
by design.

STREAMING

Elemental beauty of the moon-mark on the Baltic:
Humpty Dumpty gibbous in the water.
We've been for drinks and dinner,
dinner. Now I'm up on Deck 15, feeling full
and jogging off the appletinis. Flan.

Petersburg is in the offing – Neva, the Bolshaya Neva,
Nevsky Prospekt, Peter and Paul.
Most deliberate city in the world, wrote Fyodor.

There's a correspondence of avarice and loss. As if it
were streaming.

Behind us hale Helsinki with her church hewn
out of rock. Consonant with feeling full –
this image of a near completeness: gazing up at empty
heaven filling with careening stars, pinning wish
on wish on wish. Until the falling

                stops. Returning to la lune – he's she
now – peeping from behind a cloud, her Fabergé
an eggshell in the ripples, thin and rich – consonant,

and not. We watched the Romanovs' death before dinner.
Tsar and son were murdered first. Alexandra next.
The duchesses all sundered. Jewels the girls had sewn
into their corsets worked as mail. Bullets volleyed off
their chests like hail (which spooked the
executioners). Bayonets were used to skewer, rifle
butts to crush their skulls. – I'm not saying it
happened this way,
this is the way the movie went.

Then we went for appletinis. After that, for dinner. Flan.

Eggs again for Baby, wrote the unsuspecting empress
at the end of her summer day. *Played bezique
with Nicholas. To bed, 15 degrees.*

These nights, July, aren't dark enough for seeing stars
and comets. Chandelier-like pieces.

Hints of absolute
          passing to fragment. Oval moon now out of sight.
Midnight sky, the Gulf of
Finland – opal.

A SOLITARY GIRL IMAGINES THE BATTLE

Blue stones from the Welsh mountains.
Strangely-shaped.

Dragged to a select domain, relating to the river.

The stones, moved whole,
leave holes to be deciphered.

What do you imagine happened downstream,
nearly two miles from the procession starting-point.

After the stones are laid and raised.

So much has been spent constructing a plausible plot.

Ashes on human ashes and great strange stones.

The Avon flows from its Naseby source,
                    through the English midlands
to adjoin the River Severn at Tewkesbury town.

On the other side a girl looks
        down the eastern slope of a hill,
                past the road that runs by the river,
                    onto the olden killing ground
known as Bloody Meadow.

AGE OF THE SENTIENT SOUL

Between Sabbath and sabbath the world wobbles
on a dipstick. She smokes smoke after smoke
but her hair never smells. Hums a tune by an indie
singer, *Oh, Oh, Oh, how I've done myself in,*
blowing loopy "o"s at the orchid. A tune she's been
crooning for weeks, perched like a bird on a buckeye.
Mother's music spread on the floor – a hush
that burns but is not consumed. Helps herself
to censer and purge. Falls to her knees and skewers
the wound. Wherever she steps she touches the autoharp.
It's no secret. The body feeds on contraband bluff,
and longs to be luscious.

INTO IT

Our bodies flush with coming off the long,
cold evening walk. Duck beneath the serviceberry,
pick a colour up – a leaf, a gleam.

I call you horse, I call you trunk. You call me
back to see a tabby eating half a hardened crow –
proud predation here in quiet corner.

A singer on the limb above us tips our eyes
to him, it's him, its hymn, and then the hot-spot
on my forehead wheels – a nova –

fire-light to touch. Do I tell you, do I tell,
I tell so very little but you know this much
and many things I simply intuit. Last midnight

on our walk I saw a fat cat cross the street
and squeeze beneath the fence where Max
the whippet lives. Cat is going to get surprised

a step from now, I say, by Max. No, you counter,
Max will be inside this time of night. Just then
a screech and howl, and it is clear the two have met.

MILLEFLEURS, KOPERNIK LODGE

We sit beneath the awning, three, assimilating sun.
        He fibs: The trip to Banff was cancelled
due to stormy weather. We laugh at this,
the pad of cheese
he draws from the well of his pocket;
a box of wooden matches, gum, a plum,
                                a bent cigar.

My heart grows round, enfolds us in clematis-
    petalled pink, the warmth
                        glows rose.
He's living near the end of the road, the garden
twining vines.
A hummingbird ascends into the breeze
without a whirr, dogwood and delphiniums stir.

We say the things that people say at the height of a
glorious day. Members of a former family
finally feeling winsome.   That was what I wanted:
to conjure the quiet triumph of wisteria turning purple.

CROW POEM

The crone claws of Kafka's Prague,

Altstätder home that burned to the ground –
all except the portal. What about the Turk,

the Jew, the Skeleton and Vanity – figures
flanking the golden orrery, astronomical clock

across the Square: Did crowds assemble then
as well – waiting for the doors to part, apostles

to appear like sudden cuckoos at the strike of
the hour. Sparks fly up. The work of purification.

How hard to enter the lawful law, false to be
intended for the bourgeois bourgeoisie. Had he

been sufficiently well, he might have stayed
on Alchemists' hill. *It is not necessary to*

leave the house. Remain at the table and wait,
don't even wait. Be still, wholly alone, the

world will writhe, revealed, at your feet. In
1917 the landlord cancelled the writer's lease.

By August he was hemorrhaging. Doctor
diagnosed *catarrh of the apex of the lung. Apex*

is cozy, Franz wrote to Ottla – *something like*
saying piglet when you mean swine. If you seek,

appropriate him – start with his skeletal face.
Kafka's poetology: a living thanatology. Buried

before his parents, before his sisters were trans-
ported east, turned to earth and ash and streamed

to Lethe.   Consider how unread we'd be
if Brod had been obedient and burned the

unpublished work of his prescient friend.

POST-CROW

There are Gregors of various shapes in the basement.

I feed them Hansel/Gretel morsels,

play for them Scriabin, Glass.

Give them shelter,

spare the swatter. Lest they metamorphose

back –

into the thin somnambulist whose ever-ending sentences

maneuver me like *Sturm und Drang* in dreams.

ALEMBIC

Memory sticks to syllables, as if in poems
float human faces: here Emanuel, here Elyse –
in shield and cone and cypress. Marion in snowy
air, Phineas in fortress. Hear them in association
speak. Loquaciously in company and scrying
into I. Memory sticks to syllables – like scent
to soul, art to illness, alchemy to metal,
blood and roses. Image the alembic.

Snowy air, meet cone and shield, be fortress now
for one another; cypress. Here I am in cell
and pinnate – sticky to the touch, attar to taste.
Invisible, except to keen perceivers. The colours
of the spectrum blend in indigo, through blue.
They could have stopped at soul alone, yet moved to
cross the benedictory threshold: don't you know –
the smallest act contains a whole world view.

CORFU

We sipped lattes on the terrace of the Liston,
overheard *al-hamdu-lillah,* understood the long
cicada song. Chorus of the green cicadas chirring
their repeating theme: last two weeks of life on earth –
symphonically, in sun. We were sipping lattes,
hot white froth, September wind. Had come down
from the stone Old Fortress, fanning our faces
with tourist brochures. Walked across the town
to see St. Jason and St. Sosipater – church –
which made me think of filial love, the deeds of it
we're taught to keep, like time and even keel.

I recalled the book by Gerald Durrell, story of his boy-
hood years here – pet gull Alecko, gecko Geronimo,
Quasimodo the pigeon. Dying cry of blue-green millions
mating in the trees. I bought a card at a kiosk the size of
a dime, asked the keeper how to say cicada in modern
Greek – Tzitziki he wrote on a scrap from a sandwich
bag. I kept the word, its tune – to use in a poem
of paradise. How could it be otherwise? The pure horizon,
equal sea. We took position on the terrace – heads bent,
hands clasped, sipping and listening, *al-hamdu-lillah.*
Something like hovering, inside out.

CORONA

Take the con from fusion and you're left with
blend and melt. The old mime just lies there.
Flexed and simultaneously limpid. The kiss of
death is not about death – Dan has called it kitsch.
Sure was sweet that night we took the stoppers out,
whickered our way through the fields on our knees.
Indistinguishable from happiness, actually.
Can't, don't, shouldn't. Easy does it won't be
used against you. Same as you, I reached the peak
of secrets – all-ye-all-ye-outs-in-free came sunsetting
together, fused as a choir of vuvuzelas. The gonfalons
fell, the colours quelled, and I was going to say,
Drop me too, but you weren't about to surrender
to bets. And when the ring came up for renewal,

master would not be decoupled from it. During
the heydays sparrows drew near enough to nuzzle,
robins flew amen under the protective net and
cherry pits later lined the lintel. The window rattled
madly and the paper on the table fluttered open
to a feature on *The New Brutalism* – just as I'd been
listening to that bolshy Burgess classic in the car.
Oranges on the still-life plate turn turquoise underneath
and *Turkish Women Bathing* appear in a poem on
Delacroix. A cross will look like the letter "t" to a child
not raised in this faith. Once the clock ticks two we'll
press together. Our swans' long feathered necks entwine
like the lives of their Ithacan namesakes: Penelope
and O. I need to feel this round as well. Yes –

as in repeat. The leg of your presence reaching me
beneath the nuptial sheets. Forgive me now for every
night I spurned you because of your breath. Stars,
little collectives in the cupola; rake them in. Moon,
that dapper manikin, Mapper Danikin, pleased
as Puck. Take me to the dipper – great old ladle, blink
and switch, like lavender in the valley turning lilac
with the wind. You'll never be as scrutable as furniture
and pets. But gaps are being spanned – at Revelstoke
and Sauk-Suiattle, Skookumchuk and Bridal Veil.
Mood Street, Salvation Creek, Dog Mountain, Bridge
of the Gods. River green because of the trees. Strips of
shine striating the road – like water in the desert – lift,
and swallows mince the air with whetted wings. The
Gorge has opened wide as *agape* – stretching in cahoots.

RED, WHITE, BLACK AND BLUE

Here again – the same surprise – he peals and leads me
to the tree. I imitate him raucously we enter into song.
He's red and red is restive; I am white.

The look you gave me – old as water-earth,
as ultramarine. I felt no apprehension stepping in.
It was shallow at the littoral, as physical
as skin. But what we long for more than this

                          is sway.
I was in for quite some time – till moonlight
superseded day and lapis turned to black. Gills
were not forthcoming, so I quit and came up
plumbed. The water bears no scent of me at all now –

                          water won't.
No trace that I was ever there and gone.

Underneath this scrub-board sky of rippled-red
and blue tonight, I'm writing.
Poetry, you told me once, is proxy.

EDGEWATER

From out on the Sound, goose-song
rolls in, nasal and naughty, to shore.

Seasons turn, headstrong as instinct.
Here goads spring's paw on the pond –

prodding ice, peeking beneath.
All the same new again.

A jay shakes snow from a willow limb,
thin fizz tinkles the water.

The awe in pond soft as spawn.
Teacher, keep the key –

the ankh that brought your gaze
to mud and rushes.

GREENER

Days ago came April
snow still crusted on the patio
and ten-below wind blowing.

I see him perched a leg away – honeycombed
in cedar-weave,
and centre on his Stop-red
                                    feather-best.
My irises respond with greener green.

I was feeling low,
he seems to know,
                    but now I'm bucking up.

                    – Cardinals don't often rest this close to
house and ground.
            Cardinals don't usually
leap this near.
                    Next they could be cackling,
like crows. For now though this one's
doubling as relief. If he weren't,

I wouldn't be believing.

EVERY KIND OF KINDNESS

Mind comprises tales of snakes and amazements.
Snakes are kept concealed. Amazements
make me pray. I have no altar but my table.
Sacrifice is every time I battle and have to relent.
At these points I know nearness. I'm at the Mercy
whenever I fly. At all other times as well.
Which means pride is a flamboyance that unseats me,
the human corpse utterly vulnerable. Those who
wash and shroud it for earth or burning
know its unsayable shyness.
Then there are the boons: bees, babies, bird's-
egg blue. Aurora borealis and australis. Elements
and temperaments. Speech and laws, the ethers.
Sun creeping from brow to crown. Kindness, every kind.
For instance – ageing.

ART SOMETIMES MAKES ME VAGUE

Some day we'll live in the sky, Birdine. The big idea.
With wings. For now, and now is a very long time,
we're handed. Our food goes in and out, like the
food of the cock and hog. It's a ruddy life, Birdine –
all meat, sweat and mess. Sometimes I'd welcome
the salt self – stilled and crystal. Would trade in the
black jacket of ambition for a place to head my rest.
We're in the school of startled night, Birdine –
nobody owns it though everybody stocks a piece.

I saw a drawing the other day and cut it out of
a flyer. Been looking into it since, as if in a Möbius
Strip. A bowman looming on the left – the west –
curving down and out, meets something slanting up
like the nape of a whale. Blue glinting through its
black. Unfastened. A firebird, jet-red, Birdine, comes
plummeting unto yellow. I feel the heat of electric
mettle drawing me onto its crossroads. There isn't
any screen. Where would the firebird be, Birdine,
if it weren't affixed to this picture I've taped in my
blank book   to stay me away from answers.

HOSPITAL OF LOVE

A rock lamp lights the way of a frog in the pond.
Frog, one ribbet. Toad, one pulse.
Fish and turtles underlit,
                    the blur of murky water.
We came here
worn, red with distress.
The rock lamp flickers leaf,
        frog-green,
then greenish. Toad on the stump – a pulse, an impulse:
                            Listen for the fish.
Turtle lifts his sock-like head, casts a sidelong
glance at the past.   Not much more than this.

The pond air fractures us less and less.
The water, phlegmatic,
                can do no harm. A young and gangly
goose lifts off,
        plies his might at flying.

NOTES

"Starting With the Cardinal": "Seidel" is American poet Frederick Seidel whose collection, *Ooga-Booga* (Farrar, Straus and Giroux: 2006), I was reading at the time of writing this piece; the musicality of the name Seidel appealed to me and made its way into the poem. The allusion to "candescent beams / and horns" refers to Michelangelo's Moses, who is horned, likely because the artist relied on a translation of the Hebrew Bible in which "rays of light" around the prophet's face after his meeting with God on Mount Sinai were rendered as "horns." The word *karnaiim* in Hebrew means both "rays" and "horns"; "horns of light" is a mistranslation of *karnei-ohr* ("rays of light") that gave rise to commonplace representations of Moses horned.

"Two by Two" is for Odette.

"Years Later, Ashbery": This piece was kindled by four lines in the poem "Landscape (after Baudelaire)" by John Ashbery from his collection *A Wave* (The Viking Press: 1981:7): "Then dream of gardens, of bluish horizons, / Of jets of water weeping in alabaster basins, / Of kisses, of birds singing at dawn and at nightfall, / Of all that's most childish in our pastoral."

"On Editing" is for Catherine Black.

"Hammered Frames" is for Leigh Raney Mellor. The description of Ezekiel's angels is drawn from the Book of Ezekiel, 1:4-7: "They had the figures of human beings. However, each had four faces, and each of them had four wings; the legs of each were fused into a single rigid leg, and the feet of each were like a single calf's hoof ..." (*The JPS Hebrew-Tanakh*, The Jewish Publication Society of America: 1999).

Veil painting is a method developed by Austrian-born philosopher Rudolf Steiner (1861-1925), wherein watercolours are diluted and applied one layer at a time over dried colour, allowing an image to arise out of the interplay of colour and negative white space.

St. John's wort is a flowering perennial herb of the genus name *Hypericum perforatum*, commonly used to treat depression. Euphorbia, the botanical name for spurge, is a plant group with unisex flowers and purgative properties.

"Phthalo" is for Helena Hartman.

"Re: Collage, Searching for a Name Thereof" is for Regine Kurek.

"Ugly Stuff": The phrase "The porcelain quota," which sparked this piece, is cryptic. I offer this gloss: Under Frederick the Great of Prussia (1712-1786), Jewish couples, on the occasion of marriage, were obliged to purchase a quota of china from the china factory in Berlin. The purchase was not of their choice, but that of the factory manager, who used the opportunity to dispose of unmarketable merchandise. It was in this way that the German-Jewish philosopher, Moses Mendelssohn (1729-1786), grandfather of the composer Felix Mendelssohn (1809-1847), became the owner of twenty life-size porcelain apes, some of which are still in the Mendelssohn family. I first read of the bizarre porcelain quota in a story by Shira Nayman in *Awake in the Dark* (Scribner: 2007). For a poetic treatment of the subject, see *The Porcelain Apes of Moses Mendelssohn*, by Jean Nordhaus (Milkweed Editions: 2002).

"Two in Raluca's Waiting Room" is for Karen Perlmutter.

"What's Become of Us" is written in the manner of Robert Pinsky's poem "Antique" from *Gulf Music* (Farrar, Straus and Giroux: 2007).

"Streaming": The line *Most deliberate city in the world* attributed to Fyodor Dostoevsky, is quoted in Wikipedia (http://en.wikipedia.org/wiki/ Society_and_culture_in_Saint_Petersburg). *Eggs again for baby* and *Played bezique with Nicholas. To bed, 15 degrees* were among the last words written by Tsarina Alexandra, hours before the imperial family were executed; recorded in *Last Diary of Tsaritsa Alexandra*, by Vladimir Koslov and Vladimir Krustalev (Yale University Press: 1997).

"Age of the Sentient Soul": The line *Oh, Oh, Oh, how I've done myself in* is from the song "Sugar and Spice" by Basia Bulat on *Heart of My Own* (Secret City Records: 2010).

"Millefleurs, Kopernik Lodge" is for my parents.

"Crow Poem": "Kavka" is the Czech word for jackdaw, a small crow. Franz Kafka was born July 3, 1883 in Prague – then the Bohemian capital of the Austro-Hungarian Empire – into a Jewish family of German culture. He died of tuberculosis on June 3, 1924, having instructed his friend and literary executor, Max Brod, to destroy all his unpublished works. Brod felt unable to comply and instead devoted his life to publishing almost everything Kafka wrote, starting with the unfinished novels, *The Trial*, *The Castle*, and *Amerika*, and including diaries, notebooks, stories, and correspondence. The lines: *It is not necessary / to leave the house. Remain at the table and wait – / or don't even wait. Be still, wholly alone, / the world will writhe, revealed, at your feet* echo lines from aphorism 109 of *Franz Kafka: The Zürau Aphorisms*, translated by Michael Hofmann (Schocken Books, 2006). The lines *catarrh of the / apex of the lung. Apex is cozy . . . something like saying piglet when you mean swine* are drawn from Kafka's letter of August 29, 1917 to his sister Ottla; in *Letters to Ottla and the Family*, translated by Richard and Clara Winston, edited by Nahum Glatzer (Schocken Books, 1982).

"Post-Crow": "Gregors" alludes to Gregor Samsa – the protagonist in Franz Kafka's novella, *The Metamorphosis* – whose transformation into some kind of huge insect/vermin ("ungeheueren Ungeziefer") is related in the opening sentence; *The Metamorphosis and Other Stories*, a new translation by Joyce Crick (Oxford University Press, 2009). "*Sturm und Drang*" – literally "storm and yearning" – is also the name of a late eighteenth-century German literary and musical movement in which extremes of emotion were given expression, in response to the perceived restraints of Enlightenment rationalism.

"Corfu": *al-hamdu-lillah* is Arabic for "Praise to God" – similar to the Hebrew "Hallelujah." The book by Gerald Durrell referred to in the poem is *My Family and Other Animals* (Viking Press: 1957).

"Corona": "the kitsch of death" is drawn from Dan Chiasson's poem "... and yet the end must be as 'tis" in *The Afterlife of Objects* (The University of Chicago Press: 2002).

ACKNOWLEDGEMENTS

My thanks to the editors of the following publications in which poems in this collection first appeared, some in slightly different iterations:

The Antigonish Review: "Manicure"; *Canadian Literature*: "Embouchure"; *Carousel*: "Styx"; *Contemporary Verse 2:* "Fishing With Dean Barlow," "Into It," "Art Sometimes Makes Me Vague" in English and French; *Ditch, the poetry that matters*: "On Editing," "Ugly Stuff"; *Dream Catcher* (UK): "Woodpecker in Capricorn"; *Existere*: "Hierarchies"; *The Fiddlehead*: "Moonshine," "Phthalo," "Re: Collage, Searching for a Name Thereof"; *FreeFall Magazine*: "Corfu"; *Kestrel: Journal of Literature & Art* (US): "Naked Fifth," "13 Lung Tree," "Edgewater"; *Lichen Arts & Letters Preview*: "Wicks"; *The Malahat Review*: "Pointillists"; *Misunderstandings Magazine*: "Lemniscate" 1. and 2.; *The Nashwaak Review*: "What's Become of Us"; *Other Voices*: "Streaming"; *The Paterson Literary Review* (US): "Aubade"; *Qwerty*: "Starting with the Cardinal," "A Solitary Girl Imagines the Battle"; *Rhythm Poetry Magazine*: "Veil Painting"; *Spirit Eyes and Fireflies*: "Crow Poem," "Post-Crow," "Every Kind of Kindness"; *Taddle Creek Magazine*: "Helleborus"; *The Toronto Quarterly*: "Two in Raluca's Waiting Room," "Red, White, Black and Blue"; *Vallum: new international poetics*: "Waterwheel," "Alembic"; *The Windsor Review*: "Parker's Point," "Alchemilla," "Millefleurs, Kopernik Lodge."

Many thanks to Antonio D'Alfonso, Michael Mirolla and Connie McParland at Guernica Editions, to my writing colleagues John Oughton, Mary Lou Soutar-Hynes, Sheila Stewart, Clara Blackwood, Rosemary Blake, Merle Nudelman, Julie Roorda, Karen Shenfeld and Marianne Paul, to my translator Stéphanie Roesler, and to my mother – everyone needs an indefatigable advocate. Deep gratitude to my husband Menachem Wolff.

Printed in June 2011
by Gauvin Press,
Gatineau, Québec